How To Stop Being A Hoarder

The Ultimate Guide on How To Stop Hoarding

Patrick Anna

Copyright © by **Patrick Anna**

Table of Contents

Chapter 1

Understanding Hoarding

We imbue items with our emotions and thoughts, and we are responsible for their meaning. So, what you consider rubbish may not be junk in the view of others. And your broken toaster, which you threw away yesterday, can breathe new life into someone else's broken toaster with the pieces still functional.

What I'm trying to express is that definitions and perceptions do not make the difference. It's how your exercise impacts your life that matters. People who collect Santas have transformed their homes into functional museums for Santa-related souvenirs and goods, including bed covers, shelves full of figurines, thematic silverware, dishes, and mugs. There are even clubs for collectors.

And that's okay; these people are collectors who have discovered their love. They discovered what makes them happy and turned it into a passion. We do this because people are naturally motivated to act in ways that make them happy. Here's where the border is. Hoarders don't acquire stuff because they enjoy it, but because they dislike not doing it. A hoarder is motivated not by enthusiasm, but by the worry and aggravation he experiences when he does not.

Researchers have discovered a substantial correlation between hoarding and Obsessive Compulsive Disorder. Depending on the study, 18% to 40% of persons with OCD also exhibit symptoms of hoarding. And it's only natural, given how similar their thinking processes are.

OCD is a compelling action motivated by the fear of negative consequences if the action is not performed. Some people scrub their skin off in an attempt to achieve perfect hygiene. And they have a good reason for doing so: they are concerned about what will happen if they do not maintain a sterile degree of cleanliness. They are concerned that germs will enter and pose a health risk to themselves or their family members. That fear is precisely what drives them to extremes. Most cases of OCD involve some form of precaution. Hoarding is very similar.

Hoarders often explain their difficulty in parting with goods or throwing away garbage in four ways:

> *This is a keepsake from a significant event or person in my life, and I will never part with it.*
> *Why toss away the prospect of those products becoming worth a fortune in the future?*
> *What if I toss this away now but later realize I need it?*
> *Why throw something away when it's absolutely excellent and working?*

All of these, and more not named, are the negative repercussions that hoarders worry will occur if they do not give up their habit. Sometimes there is just compulsive fear over parting with an object, or an addiction if you will. You know you're damaging your life, that you're just pumping pure poison up your arm, but if you don't do it, you feel nothing. You feel as if you shouldn't exist. It hurts so badly that you decide to go ahead and shoot another one.

This is what defines the disease. The merciless, compulsive, and overwhelming desire to achieve something, as well as the devastation caused by not doing it. Chaos is viewed in a new way; it is tranquil, soothing, and appealing. You know it's not ordered, but how can you be sure when it's so awful, dark, and lonely? And if you are, how long before you lose track of what you know?

Hoarding, like any other condition, can be caused by a variety of things in your life. The American Great Depression of the 1940s is said to have integrated hoarding into people's daily lives. Because of the great poverty and famine, families grabbed everything they could and used and reused it to the fullest extent possible. All of this was motivated by the reality that if they did not live in this manner, they would most likely die since they lacked the necessities of life.

Clothing was worn, patched, and then worn again. Then they were passed down to future generations, and the cycle continued until the very fabric could no longer support itself. Even yet, it was used in other fabric-based items rather than being discarded.

Even now, you can see evidence of hoarding in orphan children from really poor and disadvantaged households. You see, because they know they have nothing, they never pass up an opportunity to acquire something more. Even if they don't need it right now, the future may require it, and they must be prepared. Consider prepared for the apocalypse. Their apocalypse is their reality, and they live in it.

Emotional trauma like that might create a profoundly distorted perception of priorities. Even though their apocalypse has ended, they will never be able to move on from their destructive ways.

Hoarding is also thought to be a coping mechanism for the loss of a close person in your life. You've probably seen the repercussions of obsessive hoarding before. Countless photos, articles, and films depict what it's like to be inside such people's "homes". There are even TV series about hoarders, which seem as unpleasant as making money off of other people's troubles and illnesses. You've seen the waste piles that obstruct most of the house, including the toilets, kitchens, and bathrooms. You've witnessed how people react to the stink of tens of animals living uncontrollably and uncared for. You've seen how a fridge appears when the "food" inside has liquefied. Yes, it is quite the terror.

Hoarding is just another mental disorder that, with the right care and support, can be dealt with, controlled, and even overcome. Most cases reported in the press, however, are the result of paying little attention to the problematic individual. And by zero, I mean that only 5% of all hoarders receive the attention of professionals who can assist them. Nearly half of them drop out of any rehabilitation program. It's not because the medicines are ineffective. On the contrary, after only a few weeks in such programs, patients show a 45% reduction in their hoarding behaviors.

Scientists have discovered that the earliest signs of hoarding can be detected as early as 10 years old, allowing them to intervene and treat the problem at an early stage. Illnesses do not have the capacity to heal themselves from nothing. On the contrary, if you ignore it, you can be certain that it will become larger, stronger, and more difficult to eliminate. Unattended hoarders lose control of their position by the age of thirty, and the awful examples I discussed earlier can be seen by the age of fifty.

The landlord walks into your apartment one day and throws a fit over what he finds. Naturally, rather than assisting, he has you expelled and on the streets, for example. He hires removal crews to clear the mess and then end-of-tenancy cleaners to finish the job. It may take a few weeks, but once he has a new tenant who is not sick, everything will return to normal for him.

You become the youngster who never had anything and simply delve further into the infatuation. That same preoccupation is your only companion and survival weapon, so you stop struggling for control and simply let go.

However, hoarders are not mindless. Some, if not the majority, are aware of their condition and are considerably more knowledgeable about it than everyone else. They understand what motivates them and know they desire to be free of that fixation. However, in order to succeed, they require a pleasant and helpful hand.

Facts About Hoarding

The International OCD Foundation also predicts that one out of every fifty persons suffers from obsessive and severe hoarding. This sounds like an interesting psychological topic to explore.

Anything can be hoarded

Newspapers, mail, items of clothing, household books, and trash are some examples. Serious hoarders may obsessively collect animals, food, and human garbage. Some analysts believe there are five levels of hoarding. As someone progresses through the levels, their obsession becomes more extreme. The greater the number, the poorer the standard of living. A level one hoarder, for example, has access to every door and staircase in their home. A level five hoarder lives in a home with significant structural deterioration, possibly no utilities, a broken toilet system, hazardous living conditions, and so on.

Many specialists support the Psychological Ownership Theory

The Psychological Ownership Theory is when an individual has the idea of "It's mine! This concept is applicable to many of us, but hoarders experience it on a deeper level. Essentially, this approach promotes mental ownership, personal identity, and emotional commitment to possessions. When someone has hoarding behaviors, they are too sentimental. This means that they see their belongings as an extension of who they are and what they require to feel safe. This hypothesis is intended to emphasize the severity of the emotions underlying hoarding.

There is no particular reason for hoarding

Hoarding is not like chicken pox. You don't simply catch it. Hoarding has no definite etiology because, as previously said, it is not a physical disorder. However, there are several scenarios that can be identified. Once these are identified, it is easy to determine where the disorder came from. Deep-seated familial difficulties, an innate difficulty making decisions, a terrible life experience, being raised by a hoarder, and other factors may all play a role.

These options are all included under the umbrella term "attachment theory". An attachment theory describes how someone struggles to control things in their lives. When someone hoards, they may struggle to maintain emotional control. When they keep all of these things close, they are seeking to regulate their emotions.

Hoarding can have varying degrees of intensity
Hoarding has become somewhat of a television and online sensation. You may have watched the show about the extremely interesting lives of hoarders. If not, you might be new to comprehending the illness! Our argument here is that a hoarder is more than just someone who accumulates items. Hoarders are not packrats. While the disease can have various degrees of severity, it is a serious condition.

Treatment exists, but many people do not seek it out
Hoarders often feel humiliated about their valued items. As previously stated, this is incorrect. This is not a collection that this individual is proud to display in a glass chest. Hoarders experience obsessive thinking, which results in clutter, an unpleasant living environment, and emotions of humiliation and grief. As a result, hoarders rarely seek treatment for themselves. This may also be linked to the notion that hoarders are often lonely and isolated individuals. There may be no one with a different perspective encouraging treatment. However, if treatment is desired, cognitive behavioral therapy is the preferred option. Because this is a psychiatric condition, cognitive therapy is recommended.

Hoarding may involve tangible items, but it is a psychological behavior
A hoarder is someone who has a continual need to keep stuff. These "things" might literally mean anything. While these objects and items are actual, the desire we're discussing is a psychological disease. When someone hoards, they experience psychological tension. The stress of having to get rid of an object is simply too much, which eventually leads to hoarding. People suffering from this disease are frequently unconcerned about how their surroundings look or how impractical their lifestyles have become. Their will to hoard outweighs all of this.

There is no treatment for hoarding
Hoarding is a psychiatric problem with therapeutic options. However, there is no treatment for hoarding disorder. However, there is medication available for hoarding-related symptoms. Anxiety and depression exacerbate hoarding behavior. If these diseases are treated with appropriate medication, someone's hoarding may become less life-threatening.

Most hoarders are adults, although the behavior begins in infancy
Hoarding tendencies emerge in early infancy. These traits, however, do not often manifest themselves until a person reaches adulthood. This could be because youngsters are unable to purchase their own items yet. They do not have their own home to furnish. They are being supervised and asked to clean, among other things. While a child's tendencies have not yet manifested themselves, this is where they begin. The idea of feeling attached to objects, often known as "Attachment Theory" or "Early Anxious Attachment," develops in childhood.

Hoarding has been connected to anxiety and sadness
Anxiety and despair are typically associated with hoarding behavior. Hoarders, on the other hand, are more likely to suffer from anxiety and sadness. When someone exhibits characteristics of hoarding, they are typically nervous. They may have considerable anxiety over getting rid of items. To remedy this, they collect far too many items. And, as you can expect, this just increases worry and despair. When someone is worried and unhappy, clinging to the things that make them feel secure and less lonely might lead to hoarding behavior.

Hoarders are usually persons who are extremely afraid of the world
As we noted earlier, hoarders value their excessive possessions for a reason. It may not be for the tangible objects and items themselves, but rather for the emotions that they evoke. These things can help them feel safe. These items can help them feel less alone. Typically, people with hoarding disorders are miserable, alone, and lonely. Inner attachment troubles develop when individuals are continuously surrounded by things that cause them to experience fewer of these deep sentiments. People suffering from OCD may find the world frightening. Hoarding is one of the coping strategies for this.

Chapter 2

The Consequences of Hoarding

A major source of contention emerges when hoarding results in a loss of useful living space, particularly in communal spaces such as the kitchen, living room, etc. Spaces are being used as intended, including the ability to use furniture, appliances, counters, and other items routinely and without interruption from clutter.

Another source of contention is the financial pressure that can arise from excessive purchasing in order to acquire additional items, as well as the potential necessity for storage facilities. Both can lead to debt. In addition to the potential stress, expenditures are frequently not discussed, credit cards may be "maxed out," and money cannot be allocated to goods that family members may need or want.

A third source of conflict can arise when a person with Hoarding Disorder "claims" areas of the home as their own, filling it with hoarded objects and regulating how the space is used. This involves claiming authority over the management of hoarded items and refusing to allow other family members to make decisions on their homes. This can cause feelings of helplessness, irritation, wrath, and vulnerability among family members.

Finally, conflict may emerge if family members become so annoyed with the hoarding that they attempt to clean or organize the home, particularly if they do so without the individual with a Hoarding Disorder. This conduct may cause the person with Hoarding Disorder to feel tricked or violated, resulting in family disagreements and a loss of trust.

The Spouse

Spouses of persons with Hoarding Disorder generally accept their partner's hoarding behavior for years before concluding they can't take it anymore. When their partner doesn't improve the mess despite their frequent demands, frustration and resentment gradually escalate. When a partner becomes very frustrated or the family quarrel becomes too heated, they may consider separation or divorce.

If the family has children, a custody struggle may arise. Often, images of the home are taken to court to persuade the judge that the home environment is unsuitable for raising a child. The parent with Hoarding Disorder experiences shame, remorse, and/or resentment, which interferes with their ability to raise the child together.

In rare circumstances, both members of the couple exhibit hoarding tendencies and fill their homes with objects that each thinks necessary. In such instances, intervention is unlikely to be effective unless both couples agree to work on the problem together.

The Children

Children of persons suffering from Hoarding Disorder are frequently unable to avoid living amid extreme clutter, particularly if they are minors, which has an impact on their social lives and development. Children are frequently too embarrassed by all of the things to invite friends over, or they are forbidden to do so because of their parents' humiliation. This may cause feelings of loneliness, powerlessness, and resentment. In severe circumstances, children may not have enough space to play or study, prompting child protective authorities to investigate the parent who hoards.

Children may also be resentful, despondent, or angry about the lifestyle their parents' Hoarding Disorder forces them to live. Children may grow to think that their guardians with Hoarding Disorder appreciate their stuff more than their children, which can lead to feelings of abandonment, rejection, and/or that they are not loved or treasured as much as their parents' belongings.

Because of the increasing family strife, children may be pulled between the parent with a Hoarding Disorder and the one without it. If the family disagreement escalates to the point where divorce is considered, children may blame the person with a Hoarding Disorder for the family breakdown.

Legal concerns may emerge if a neighbor becomes aware of the scenario and contacts Child Protective Services (CPS). If this occurs, an investigation may be initiated, which may end in the removal of children from the family, unless one of the parents provides alternative living arrangements. Whether the child continues to live amid extreme clutter or is removed from the house, the consequences can be disastrous for the family.

Adult children suffering from hoarding disorder may have bad relationships with their parents. As adult children leave the house, they may become alienated from their parents who have Hoarding Disorder owing to arguments over how to handle hoarding. Adult children may also blame their parents for the conditions they experienced as youngsters. Parents of young children may be anxious about their safety in a cluttered grandparent's home. As a result, grandparents may become alienated from their grandkids, causing not just distance within the family but also further isolation for the individual with Hoarding Disorder.

Adult offspring of those with Hoarding Disorder may encounter a condition known as "caregiver burden," which occurs when people are compelled to provide emotional or practical care for somebody else. Being a caretaker may result in greater interpersonal conflict, chronic concern, anxiety, sadness, and incapacity to cope. Caregivers may also face a variety of unpleasant life events, including low self-esteem, financial instability, loss of competence, loss of hope and security, and trouble planning for the future.

Health and Safety at Home

Beyond the emotional implications, Hoarding Disorder can have an influence on family safety and health; the impacts of hoarding affect all members of the household, not just the person with the disorder. As clutter accumulates, it becomes increasingly difficult to eliminate commonly collected dust, pet hair, pollen, filth, and other contaminants from the home because members of the family are unable to vacuum or dust for months or longer. Additionally, spilled fluids cannot be cleaned, resulting in mildew, fungus, and/or unwelcome bugs. People with Hoarding Disorder and their families may suffer from headaches, breathing issues, and allergies as a result of the poor living conditions in their homes. The inability to clean can also cause bathrooms in the home to become unusable or so cluttered that the toilet, sink, and/or shower are inaccessible. Thus, cleanliness for the entire family may become a concern.

A hoarded home is often so cluttered that paths must be carved through it to go around. These pathways may get obstructed by fallen or new debris, causing individuals to trip, slip, and fall. Not only does this affect individuals who are physically capable, but excess clutter may offer an even bigger risk to anyone living in the home who is unable to move. In severe circumstances, the house may become so congested and difficult to maneuver that family members can only utilize one or two rooms.

Clutter might also interfere with safety practices. In addition to being a fire danger, clutter can prohibit family members from leaving the house in the event of an emergency and/or prevent emergency response workers from entering the house. Fire is especially dangerous when paper goods are piled high and near a stove, heater, or other flammable objects. If a fire does break out, household members may be unable to reach fire extinguishers to suppress it, and toxic fumes from combustible objects may cause additional health problems for all those exposed. Burning items may fall during a fire, posing a trapping threat and impeding firefighters' ability to rescue individuals from the home.

In homes with severe Hoarding Disorder, flooring may be unable to support the weight of excessive clutter. The weight of all the clutter, combined with the possibility of water damage from broken or clogged pipes and appliances, puts a huge amount of pressure on floorboards, causing them to rot. There are additional dangers in houses with pets. Cats may be unable to use their litter boxes, and dogs may be permitted to urinate and defecate inside the home because their owners are unable to navigate the clutter to bring them outdoors. This, combined with the possibility of mildew and fungus from spilled liquids, can attract pests, infesting the residence and rendering it uninhabitable according to public health guidelines.

Chapter 3

Addressing the Root Causes

No one understands exactly what promotes hoarding, but there are numerous hypotheses. Various individuals will have different explanations for their personal experiences. It is likely to be a combination of variables. Hoarding can be linked to challenging events and negative emotions. You may find these difficult to articulate, confront, or resolve. Some people claim that hoarding helps them manage other mental health issues or distracts them from feeling extremely nervous, disturbed, or terrified.

There can be a connection between hoarding and controlling their impulses. This is when it becomes nearly impossible to avoid certain acts, like as purchasing stuff.

Perfectionism and Worrying

If you hoard stuff, you may be overly concerned about making mistakes, commonly known as perfectionism. You may also find it difficult to make decisions, plan ahead, or figure out how to complete chores. These could be reasons why some people are more prone to hoarding.

For example, you may struggle to organize or group your belongings into categories, or to select what to keep or discard. The concept of doing this may appear so difficult or upsetting that it is preferable not to try. Sometimes I get provoked because I am concerned about the norms of society of what I should be doing or attaining.

Childhood experiences

Some studies feel that hoarding stems from childhood memories of losing things, not owning things, or not being cared for. This can involve experiences such as:

> *Growing up in poverty or with financial concerns.*
> *Having someone take or toss away your belongings.*
> *Hardship, emotional abuse, or neglect. For example, if your fundamental needs were not satisfied if people did not treat you with warmth and support.*

These memories may make you feel more connected to your belongings or make it difficult for you to manage them. My parents were full of stories about their parents and grandparents' deprivations; it was part of my perspective growing up, and I know that persistent disorganization amplifies the impact of every extra item I own.

Trauma and Loss

You might be able to trace the origins of your hoarding to a painful event in your life. This may include:

> *Being abused, bullied, or harassed, including facing racism*
> *Breaking up with your partner*
> *experiencing bodily health difficulties.*
> *Losing a person close to you.*
> *Feeling really lonely or secluded.*

Experiencing extended durations of tension or feeling very stressed

For some of us, these events may exacerbate our hoarding, especially if we began before a stressful moment. It seemed as if she had created a wall of goods to keep everyone out. Having been through various tragic occurrences in her life, including the loss of her kid, a painful divorce, her partner's heart attack, and the death of her mother. Nobody could harm her if she was safeguarded by all of this stuff.

Family historical issues

It is normal for people to emulate what they have learned from their family members. People frequently emulate the behaviors they observe others performing on a regular basis.

For example, a child may notice that mom or dad has a pattern of saving specific items. Because it's mom and dad, they accept this "hoarding behavior" as usual. When children grow up, they believe they should emulate their parents. Where this becomes an issue is when they had no idea the behavior was damaging at the time, and it still has the potential to be destructive to them today.

Here's what makes this occurrence so interesting. It is only when the clutter in their own home gets overwhelming that they realize how horrible the mess was in their childhood environment.

Is there an element of genetics involved here? While there is no proof that a "hoarding" gene is real, it is not unreasonable to believe that any psychiatric illness may have a genetic component. This is especially true when multiple family members display the same behaviors.

Chapter 4

Treatment

Successful hoarding care requires the patient to be highly motivated and committed. Attempts to clean out hoarders' homes without addressing the underlying problem typically fail. Family members and community agencies can invest many hours clearing up a home only to discover that the problem returns, frequently within a few months. Hoarders whose homes are emptied without their agreement frequently endure severe distress and may become even more connected to their stuff, potentially leading to future denial of aid. The basic therapies for compulsive hoarding are psychotherapy, medication, or a combination of the two.

Psychotherapy

Strategies for treating hoarding include confronting the hoarder's views and beliefs about the need to maintain goods and accumulate new things; going out without purchasing or picking up new items; and removing and recycling clutter. The first stage is to rehearse removing clutter with the assistance of a clinician or coach. Second, hoarders may want to discover and join a support group or collaborate with a coach to sort through and minimize clutter. The third step is to recognize that relapses may occur and devise a strategy to avoid further clutter.

Cognitive-behavioral therapy (CBT) is one treatment option for hoarding. CBT addresses four major problem areas:

> - *Information processing impairments*
> - *Problems developing emotional relationships.*
> - *Behavioral avoidance*
> - *Incorrect assumptions regarding the nature of possessions.*

CBT for compulsive hoarding is therefore focused on reducing clutter, enhancing decision-making and organizational abilities, and strengthening resistance to the want to save.

Hoarders can benefit from time-limited group cognitive-behavioral therapy (GCBT), which has been shown to ameliorate OCD symptoms. This has become a popular psychological therapy in recent years, with research papers indicating the feasibility and limited success of GCBT approaches in treating hoarding disorders. Group treatment may be particularly beneficial due to its cost-effectiveness, increased client access to professional doctors, and reduction in the social isolation and shame associated with this disease. More study is needed to increase the efficacy of GCBT approaches for hoarding, as well as to investigate the durability of change, outcome predictors, and change-influencing processes.

When a person is willing to discuss a hoarding problem, behavioral counselors often employ the following guidelines: Recognize that people have the right to make their own decisions at their own pace; realize that everyone has an attachment to their possessions; and offer suggestions for making the home safer, such as removing clutter from doorways and hallways. Counselors collaborate with clients who hoard and avoid disputing over whether to keep or remove an item. Instead, counselors determine what will drive the individual to reject items and organize. Developing trust, as well as sympathy and respect for the hoarder, is crucial.

People who hoard might be encouraged to see how their hoarding habit interferes with their aims or values. For example, if a hoarder wants a more active social life, decluttering the home may allow the person to arrange social gatherings. Cognitive rehabilitation and exposure therapy are other viable approaches to treating hoarding in older persons.

Pharmacotherapy

Studies have indicated that selective serotonin reuptake inhibitor (SSRI) medications work effectively for OCD patients, and some of these meds have also been proven to be useful in people with hoarding tendencies.

In a 2011 research of around 80 OCD patients, 32 of whom had compulsive hoarding syndrome, all subjects were given paroxetine 20 mg (Paxil) alone for an average of 80 days. Both groups responded significantly after therapy for OCD symptoms, hoarding, sadness, and anxiety; this finding contrasts prior research that found compulsive hoarding fails to respond effectively to SSRI treatment. The study indicated that SSRIs appear to be equally helpful for hoarders and non-hoarding OCD patients.

Venlafaxine is an SSRI that also acts as a norepinephrine reuptake inhibitor at higher dosages. Preliminary results with venlafaxine indicate a satisfactory response with hoarding behaviors in some people, with a trend toward a larger reduction in hoarding symptoms than with paroxetine.

New therapeutic techniques could include cognitive enhancers like donepezil or galantamine, which boost cholinergic neurotransmission in the cortex of the brain. Stimulant drugs can improve the performance of medial prefrontal cortical areas associated with attention and executive function.

Pharmacotherapy for compulsive hoarding seems to be at least as effective as cognitive behavioral treatment. It is now believed that the combination of medication and CBT for compulsive hoarding is more successful than either treatment alone.

Researchers are also looking for functional abnormalities in the brain and information-processing deficiencies that appear to underpin hoarding illness. A novel type of transcranial magnetic stimulation (TMS), a noninvasive magnetic field that stimulates nerve cells in specific parts of the brain to treat mood regulation and depression, may be effective for patients suffering from hoarding behavior.

Hoarding disorder can be associated with a variety of developmental, neurologic, and psychiatric behaviors. Clinically severe hoarding is common and can range from moderate to life-threatening.

Chapter 5

Developing a Decluttering Mindset

It is the key to a more organized home, but what precisely is a decluttering mindset? Simply described, it is the ability to let go of items that are no longer needed or used. For certain individuals, this is natural. They can look at their messy homes and promptly identify what may be given, sold, or discarded.

Others, however, find it much more difficult to let go of things. We save things because we believe we will need them someday or because they have emotional significance. However, accumulating too much stuff can lead to feelings of overload and anxiety. If you want to live a more deliberate life and clear your environment, start by developing a decluttering mindset. When you're able to get rid of the clutter in your home, you'll feel lighter, freer, and more calm. Ways to Cultivate a Decluttering Mindset

Eliminate thoughts of deprivation
One of the reasons we save things is because we believe we will need them someday. What if, instead of viewing decluttering as a deprivation, you saw it as an opportunity?

The scarcity mindset is the belief that there is not enough of a certain thing to go around. So, if you get the opportunity to get your hands on something, take it since you may not have another chance. It is frequently the outcome of living in a world of plenty. We're so used to having all we could ever desire or need that we're afraid of living without it.

However, this is not a true representation of the reality. In truth, there's plenty to go around. And once you perceive decluttering as an opportunity rather than a deprivation, it becomes much easier to let go of stuff.

Learn how to say no
Have you ever been offered a goodie bag containing random items and told 'it's free'? We have all been there. We accept the bag even though we don't need or want any of its contents. Expect additional coffee mugs, pens, and discounts.

A similar thing occurs when relatives or close friends offer to give us their old belongings. We feel compelled to say yes, even if we don't truly want or need it. If you want to cultivate a decluttering mindset, you must learn to say no. When someone gives you something you do not need or want, respectfully decline. It may be challenging at first, but the more you practice, the easier it becomes. And gradually, people will stop handing you their unwanted items since they know you won't take them.

Change your perspective
How you see decluttering can have a significant impact on your inclination to undertake it. If you consider it as an unavoidable problem, something that will consume a lot of your time and energy, it will not be a pleasant experience. However, if you shift your attitude and see it as a chance to simplify your life, it may be a lot more enjoyable experience. Consider all of the advantages of decluttering: reduced stress, increased peace of mind, and a simpler lifestyle. When you start seeing the advantages, it becomes simpler to let go of the problems.

Let go of the past
Many of us hang onto things because we are reluctant to let go of our past. We might have high school clothes or childhood souvenirs. While it's understandable to desire to keep these items, keep in mind that they're only material goods. They don't make up your identity as a person. If you're having trouble moving on from the past, consider the future. What do you envision your life to be like in five, ten, or even twenty years? Do you want to be weighed down by a lot of items, or do you want to be able to travel lightly and enjoy yourself? Keep in mind your past does not determine your future. You can let go of the past and shape the future you want for yourself.

More does not mean better
In today's world, there is a lot of tension to keep up with the Joneses. We see our neighbors and close friends with the latest technology and luxury outfits and feel compelled to keep up. Television advertisements tell us that we need to acquire new things to be happy, and we believe it.

But here's the thing: more doesn't always mean better. Just because someone owns a larger house or a fancier car does not imply that they are happier than you are. Don't fall into the trap of believing that having more items will make you happier. Instead, prioritize quality over quantity. Choose goods that will bring you delight, and let the rest go.

Develop a vision for your life
When you're feeling overwhelmed by your possessions, it can be beneficial to stand back and consider what you want your life to look like. Do you prefer to

live in a messy, chaotic home, or in a tranquil, serene environment? Creating a vision for your life might help you let go of what is holding you back. When you know what you want, it's simpler to let go of things that don't add value to your life.

Memory is not stored in things

One of the most common misunderstandings regarding decluttering is that we need to keep things because they have memories. But the truth is that memories are not kept in things, they are kept in our hearts and memories. There is no need for a physical object to remind you of a specific period in your life. Instead, consider another way to commemorate those memories. For example, you could photograph the item or record your favorite memory related to it. Alternatively, you may take a few seconds to meditate on the memories before letting them go.

Leave the guilt behind

Guilt is a common feeling associated with decluttering. We frequently feel terrible about discarding something that has been given to us, or we may believe that throwing something away is wasteful. But here's the thing: you should not feel bad about decluttering. It's your life, and you deserve to live it whatever way you want. If you feel guilty about trying to declutter, consider that the individual who gave you the thing wants you to be happy. They would not want you to keep stuff that doesn't make you happy. Gift-giving is about making the recipient happy, not the giver. So, if you're holding onto anything out of guilt, let go and enjoy the liberty that comes with it.

Forget about money

It's easier said than done, but while decluttering, try to ignore how much money you spend on an item. It can be tempting to keep something because we feel we "waste" money on it, but this is not very productive. Remember that material possessions are exactly that: material. They do not define your worth, nor do they decide your enjoyment. If you aren't getting rid of something because you spent a lot of money on it, ask yourself if you would spend that much money on it today, if the answer is no, let it go.

Mindset adjustments are key for decluttering. It is not enough to just rummage through your belongings and get rid of what you do not need. You must modify your way of thinking about things, which requires time, effort, and practice. When you adopt a decluttering mindset, the cleaning process becomes much easier. You'll begin to see your belongings in a new perspective, making it simpler to let go of those items that are holding you back. Remember that a decluttered home isn't perfect. It's a home that conveys your beliefs, interests, and lifestyle. So do not strive for perfection. Simply focus on making progress and let go of the rest.

Chapter 6

Practical Decluttering Strategies

These tactics for simplifying and practical cleansing are gradual and consistent. There is no one ideal approach to decluttering, but getting rid of everything all at once is rarely a permanent solution. Consider the significant adjustments you've made in your life. Do you do better with fast and furious or slow and steady?

I understand how frustrating it may be. Slow and steady isn't as sexy or spectacular as fast and furious, but it has certain appealing qualities. Slow and steady can be compassionate, thoughtful, and relaxing, as opposed to a more quick, stressful approach. Slow and steady offers a platform to effect change that can affect every aspect of your life, as well as the opportunity to learn and grow along the way. Try these gradual and consistent tactics for practical decluttering.

Strategies for Practical Decluttering

These practical decluttering ideas can assist you in taking a careful approach to streamlining your living environments. They'll help you avoid typical errors and gain momentum. You'll find the guidance and viewpoint you need for slow and steady tidying below, whether it's in your closet, a pile of documents, or wherever else you have too much stuff.

Stop junk from entering
Challenge yourself and your entire household to three months of just purchasing necessities and/or disposing of something every time a new item enters your home. Purchases, presents, and office or school-related products are examples of incoming items. In other words, everything matters. If you buy a new pair of sneakers, donate your old ones. If you purchase a new cosmetic product, discard the residues of previous ones, which have most likely expired. If you purchase new dishes, give away the ones you were using previously. This will help you avoid clutter creep while you're tidying.

Clearly identify the mission
There is a significant distinction between organizing and decluttering. Organizing simply involves transferring items from one location to another. Instead of striving so hard to locate the right position for anything, consider

the possibility that it no longer has a place in your home or heart. This transformation in how you think about the items in your living area will enable you to create a clutter-free environment.

Forget about it

If you keep stuff in storage, you've most likely written the contents on the exterior of each box. How would you ascertain what was contained within? Remembering what's in the box without a label is a clear indication of how significant the items are to you. Fill a box with items you aren't ready to part with but aren't sure you need. Mark the box "Waste or donate after 30 days." Then, move the package out of sight. After 30 days, if you can't remember what's in the box or don't want to open it, donate it all.

Ask for assistance

We might become so attached to our possessions that it is difficult to determine when to hang on and when to let go. We can't see the forest for the trees while wading through our own clutter. Consider decluttering tips, or ask a close companion or family member for assistance. Create a checklist and allow this person to vote "yes" or "no" on apparel, ornamental pieces, and other goods. Even better, switch services and agree to reciprocate by visiting your friend's house. Even if it feels difficult, asking for help is the simplest approach to achieving progress.

Invite everyone to the party

When you start decluttering, encourage your family to help. Don't force; instead, invite. Remember, however, that while it is easiest to seek for clutter in someone else's area, your family may feel pressured. Start with your own personal items. Allow family members to work on decluttering their belongings at their own speed. If you want others to see joy in less, you must first live cheerfully with less.

Declutter in stages

Even if you're eager to declutter your entire home, start with the simple tasks to strengthen your decluttering muscles. Items such as duplicates, ornamental items, appliances for the kitchen you haven't used in years, things you don't use or love, and objects in storage that haven't been a part of your life in a long time will be simpler to let go. Each thing you let go of strengthens and motivates you to let go of the next.

Travel with less

Use your practical decluttering skills when traveling to lighten your suitcase. Packing light is an excellent habit for living lightly. Pack for half of your next vacation's duration. Leave the "just in case" items at home, and note how much lighter you feel walking through the terminal, unpacking at the hotel, and visiting a new region without worrying about your belongings. How do you feel when you are unable to manage all of your usual responsibilities? If you enjoy your time with less, you may take the inspiration back with you and let go more easily.

Rethink sentimentality

The final stage of decluttering is typically reserved for the most difficult items, such as pricey items and objects with sentimental worth. If the pricey items serve no function in your life, sell them and use the earnings to pay off debt or contribute to charity.

If you are storing stuff to pass down to your kids, keep in mind that they most likely will not want them. If you're unsure about what your adult children want, ask them. Then believe them. Your youngsters understand that real treasures are not found in the attic or in any tangible object.

Release bad emotions

When you let go of objects you've kept because you spent a lot of money on them or made a large investment in them, try to let go of the guilt associated with poor shopping judgments and overspending. If you feel terrible about letting go, holding on, spending money, or wasting time, it's time to replace those negative thoughts with ones of appreciation. As an alternative to "I shouldn't have spent that money," try thinking "I'm thankful that I realize what's most essential to me right now."

You've already paid enough. If you don't let go of your guilt now, you'll continue to pay in time, attention, energy, and heart. The genuine cost of the products you're holding is significantly higher than the price tag.

Make way for more of the good stuff

Less clutter, debt, and distractions are what you first want less of while decluttering, but eventually, you'll want more. Make more place in your life for what you truly want, how you want to contribute to the world, and what is important to you. Make way for more nice stuff. There may be times when you have additional room before deciding what you want more of, which might seem unpleasant. Resist filling in all the blanks because there are frequent answers in the suffering, take as much time as you need.

During the cleansing process, you will realize that the "more" you seek is not about your goods and material possessions. Each of these gradual and consistent tactics for practical decluttering will allow you to create additional room, time, and love with ease rather than struggle, and joy rather than grief. Keep in mind that this new attitude is not a fast fix, but rather a long-term transformation and new perspective on your life.

Irrespective of whether you're organizing a bookshelf, junk drawer, living room, or bathroom, or embarking on a minimalist journey, remember to treat yourself and your loved ones with kindness as you learn to release the clutter while retaining the affection.

Chapter 7

Overcome Emotional Attachments

Even if you've never heard the phrase "sentimental clutter," you definitely have some in your home. Simply look for the things to which you've attached sentimental significance but don't need, use, or even like. One of the most difficult habits to break is emotional attachment to stuff like presents, souvenirs, and inherited artifacts. But, as tough as it is to give up these objects, you should not let them clutter your home or cause stress in your life. Here are some tips to help you feel good about getting rid of sentimental clutter.

Let It Move

If you're caught between dumping a sentimental object and keeping it in your house indefinitely, remember there's a third option: contribute it to somebody in need. Perhaps you have a relative or close friend who would truly appreciate and use the item, have been looking to thrift it for a while, or have a local location where you prefer to give used stuff. This ensures that it will go to a decent home.

Determine what is worth keeping

When analyzing an object, consider: What exactly am I sentimental about? It's likely that the association with a person, location, or time is more important than the object itself. You can remember something even if you don't have a physical reminder. However, if you truly love the piece, it is not cluttered and is probably worth retaining.

Remake or repurpose an item

To preserve your connection to an unusable item, build something new that keeps its sentimental worth. For example, a stone from an old ring can be reset into a more modern band, or a collection of T-shirts from memorable events can be transformed into a patchwork. It's worthwhile to make a one-of-a-kind thing that has a purpose rather than collecting dust.

Keep one of the bunch

If you have a collection of treasured objects, such as all of your childhood stuffed animals, you can save the sentimental attachment by keeping only one of the items. For example, suppose your grandmother handed you her favorite centerpiece of artificial fruit, which you recall being present at all of your family vacations. If you don't want to use it as a centerpiece, simply keep one of the pieces of fruit.

Do not let gifts become burdens

Many people keep their presents because they believe the giver will expect to see them exhibited or used when they visit. In actuality, the giver might not have expected that. Even if they do, the expectation is unfair. A gift is yours to use as you wish. So, if you want to give it away to prevent cluttering up your area, that's your choice.

Save a digital memory

When looking through documents or images, consider scanning and storing them digitally rather than keeping boxes with paper copies, except you need the original copies for a specific reason. This can free up a significant amount of physical space for storage in your home. This can also be done with three-dimensional things, like children's toys. If you no longer need the actual objects, photograph them instead of storing them.

Pass on heirlooms

If you received a family treasured possession, you are not bound to preserve it if you dislike it. Your mess could be a relative's treasure. So, before you get rid of an unpleasant inherited item or store it, check around to see whether anyone else in the family would like to have it. Additionally, depending on the treasured possession, it could be useful to a local library or history museum.

Keep a scrapbook

A scrapbook can help you organize your sentimental clutter whilst making it easily available when you wish to relive those memories. Add photos, letters, and other documents to the scrapbook. Make comments in the margins to explain their relevance. This scrapbook might one day be passed down to future generations of family.

Chapter 9

Establishing and Maintaining an Organized Space

After years of learning about the organization and experimenting with numerous approaches in my own home, I've developed a basic system that I frequently employ when organizing any part of my home. It will not occur overnight. But if we work on the clutter gradually, we'll soon feel more organized.

Take everything out of the space
You understand what they say: sometimes things have to be worse before they get better! This is generally the case when organizing. I find it beneficial, to begin with a clean slate. Clearing the entire room always allows me to see what I have. I can then assess my storage requirements and make the best use of the area.

If my room contains too many stuff
If we are arranging an entire space, removing everything at once may not be practical. In that situation, we can divide the room into smaller sections and tackle one at a time. In the cooking area, for example, we may divide the effort into three stages: organizing the refrigerator, organizing the pantry, and organizing the cabinets. Alternatively, in a bedroom, we could organize our clothes first, then our nightstands, and last the floor and/or various other surfaces. If you're feeling intimidated by the number of stuff that needs to be eliminated from a place, divide it into smaller portions and work on it gradually.

De-clutter like crazy
I strive to be as ruthless as possible while decluttering. If I haven't used something in a while, it's probably time to get rid of it. If it's broken, I toss it. And when something is stained or worn out, I know it's time to get rid of it. The more stuff we can get rid of, the less cluttered our environment will feel. We can have either the stuff or the space, but not both.

We cleared out our space and now have a wonderful blank slate in front of us. We just wish to return what is absolutely essential. I have a tendency to save things because I assume I might use them "someday." But in actuality, I use far less of my possessions than I realize. And if I'm not utilizing it, it should go.

Does the item need to be moved?
Along with selling or donating stuff, decluttering a place may also entail moving items to a more appropriate location. If we find decor pieces in the kitchen cupboards, for example, we could move them to a storage area instead. If we get rid of stuff but our closet remains full, we might move blazers to our coat closet or off-season clothing to under-bed bins.

Put the items together
As we remove items from the room and clean, we may start separating them into groups. When I organized my pantry, for example, I grouped all of my spices, canned goods, baking supplies, and so on.

When my stuff is organized by type, it is easier to see what I have. If I have duplicates or triples of items, I can declutter some of them. Perhaps I learned that some of the goods in the space would be better housed somewhere else, and I can relocate them.
Separating objects into categories also allows me to easily identify what I'm working with and select appropriate bins to contain each category.

Similar Items
Taking categorized items and figuring out how to maintain each one in a pleasant, accessible way is the next step in the organizing process. This does not require us to go out and buy a lot of sophisticated bins. I always start with what I have in the house and attempt to be innovative. I've used shoe boxes and diaper boxes wrapped in lovely paper to keep items in various places. I applied decorative tape to otherwise uninteresting bins, getting organized doesn't have to be expensive.

To take things a step further, I frequently stack bins inside of bins. Because each object has its own designated space, this helps to further control the clutter. I know that when I take stuff out and use them, they have their own location to return to, and I'm more likely to put everything back in order.

Label containers, boxes, and organizers
Labeling is not only useful for rapidly determining what is there, but it is also visually appealing! There are various ways I enjoy labeling. I occasionally print a basic tag from a system. Sometimes I use a label maker to make a label. You may handwrite a chalkboard sign.

Along with identifying the outside of my bins, I will occasionally make a list of what's inside and attach it. I did this with the containers in my condo craft closet, and it makes it considerably simpler to find what I need.

Refill the gap
Our space has been empty up until this point, but now that we've separated everything, organized it into bins, and labeled it, it's time to start returning things back. I always start with the goods I use the most and place them in the most convenient location. Items that are used infrequently can be stored on higher shelves or in other difficult-to-access areas. From there, I fill in the gaps until everything has a place, always keeping items close.

Put things back in their places
Once everything is organized and back in place, the only way it will stay that way is if we make a habit of returning things to their proper places as soon as we finish utilizing them.

Honestly, this is a struggle for me. My scatterbrained side often leaves supplies and half-finished projects lying about. I work hard to develop excellent organizational systems, so if I want to keep them, I must commit to returning items to their proper locations when I'm finished.

Add a visual indication as a reminder to maintain the organizational system
Giving ourselves a visual indication is one approach to getting into the habit of returning items to their proper locations. Start with the cooking area and put a post-it note on the refrigerator that simply says, "Put it back! Alternatively, place a similar note on the washroom mirror or closet door. New habits do not emerge overnight, but if we create clever organizing systems and make it a point to maintain them, putting things back where they belong will become second nature over time, rather than work.

Don't be frightened to replace ineffective organizational systems
I've spent a lot of time building up systems and making them appear nice, but when it comes to day-to-day use, they weren't practical or workable. When I was organizing under our sink, for example, I stacked closed boxes on top of each other. It appeared to be a neat pile, but it was difficult to get to the goods at the bottom, so I either avoided using them or made a large mess attempting to get to them.

When I realized my approach wasn't working, I was able to substitute the boxes with cabinets that I could simply pull out to grab what I wanted, which worked considerably better.

Conclusion

Living in dangerous conditions and having clutter in your house degrades your quality of life. Stress, humiliation, and anxiety are just a few of the emotions that may accompany this major mental health issue.

However, there is no reason to feel humiliated. The American Psychiatric Association (APA) estimates that 2.6% of the population suffers from hoarding disorder; prevalence and symptoms are comparable across national, racial, and gender boundaries. The resulting clutter may pose safety and health risks. It can cause mental pain in both the individual with the illness and their family and friends. Hoarding problem frequently co-occurs with other mental health issues. Knowing what hoarding disease looks like is essential to deciding whether you or a loved one needs to get help.

Signs and Symptoms of Hoarding Disorder

Saving an excessive amount of random stuff is the first indication of a hoarding problem. Clutter can accumulate over time until there is no more living space. Because this occurs over time, it may go overlooked until someone points out how cluttered a space has grown.

Symptoms of hoarding disorder can appear as early as the teenage years. Symptoms tend to worsen with time and are more difficult to treat. People with the disease continue to amass items even when they run out of space or don't need them. Because people with hoarding problems frequently keep goods in their homes, it might take some time before others notice that they are hoarding.

A lot of individuals with hoarding disorder have trouble allowing others into their houses. This can lead to isolation, exacerbating many mental health problems.

The signs and symptoms of hoarding disorder are:

- *Excessive collection of objects with little or no place to store them*
- *Difficulty giving up possessions of insignificant value.*
- *The compulsion to save goods or getting irritated if someone advises tossing them away*
- *Accumulating clutter until it becomes difficult or impossible to move in living places.*
- *Indecision, avoidance, delay, and disorganization.*

Accumulated things present a tripping risk. If there are too many goods in the way of first responders during an emergency, they may be unable to enter the home's rooms. Clutter in the kitchen or bathroom might make it difficult to cook or bathe. Trying to live in overly cluttered areas might cause stress for household members. It can also lead to conflict, as others may desire to remove objects that are significant to the hoarder.

Collecting Items Versus Hoarding

People with hoarding disorder may identify themselves as overly passionate collectors. But there are several reasons why this is untrue. Hoarding disorder is characterized by difficulties parting with any items. When someone with the disease attempts to discard stuff, they endure severe distress. As a result, they begin to acquire these items in their homes and other locations.

Collectors, on the other hand, gather and organize stuff with purpose. Collectors frequently seek out certain things that they can either pass on to others or sell for a profit. Although they may not utilize the things, they can display them for others to appreciate.

Hoarding disorder is usually impulsive, and disorganized, and rarely entails giving up stuff once gained. While not all hoarding behavior is disruptive, many persons with the disease are ashamed of the clutter in their houses and purposefully avoid showing it to others. People over the age of 60 with other mental health issues are more likely to engage in hoarding behavior. This is especially true for those dealing with despair and anxiety.

Causes of Hoarding

At this moment, experts have not identified particular causes of hoarding disorder. Nevertheless, genetics and brain function appear to play a part. According to a 2009 research in the American Journal of Psychiatry, 50% of patients with hoarding disorder have at least one relative who has the illness. In reality, many people with hoarding disease grew up in cluttered environments. Clutter may bring them comfort.

Risk Factors
Hoarding problem typically starts between the ages of 11 and 15. However, hoarding conduct is more common in elderly adults than in young adults. Some of the risk factors for hoarding disorder are:

Personality
Many individuals with hoarding disorder exhibit indecisiveness or perfectionism.

Heredity
If you have relatives with hoarding problems, you are more likely to get it as well.

Stressful life events
Triggers such as the death of someone you care about, an eviction, or a divorce may cause hoarding behavior.

Conditions Associated with Hoarding Disorder

Many people with hoarding problems have other mental health issues. According to the American Psychiatric Association, 75% of patients with the illness also suffer from a mood or anxiety issue. Other conditions that frequently coexist with hoarding disorder consist of attention deficit hyperactivity disorder (ADHD), dementia, post-traumatic stress disorder (PTSD), and obsessive-compulsive disorder (OCD).

Often, these coexisting illnesses are the primary reason individuals seek treatment before hoarding disorder is diagnosed. When a concerned family member approaches a mental health professional for help, people with hoarding disorder are more likely to receive treatment.

Individuals with hoarding disorder may avoid seeking therapy because they are ashamed of their illness. They may not realize the scope or gravity of their problem. Those suffering from hoarding disorder deserve assistance in reducing their misery and creating a healthy living environment for themselves and their loved ones.

Diagnosing Hoarding

If hoarding is interfering with a healthy quality of life or making a house unsafe, it is necessary to seek professional help. Individuals might seek diagnosis and therapy from a mental health expert to overcome hoarding behavior and live a healthy life.

A therapist meets with the person in question to discuss their symptoms before making a diagnosis and providing treatment. Hoarding disorder is diagnosed through a professional examination based on criteria from The Diagnostic and Statistical Manual of Mental Disorders: Fifth Edition (DSM-5).

Hoarding was previously included as an OCD symptom in the DSM. In 2013, the American Psychological Association (APA) defined hoarding as a separate condition. If these requirements are met, an official hoarding disorder assessment may be conducted.

> - *Difficulty discarding worthless objects.*
> - *Accumulating goods until they occupy all available living space*
> - *Feeling nervous, upset, and depressed about the prospect of giving up possessions*
> - *Using obsessive behavior to acquire, steal, or scavenge assets*
> - *Having delusional beliefs when examining hoarding tendencies.*
> - *There is no history of a brain injury or any other ailment that could explain aberrant behavior.*

Cognitive Behavioral Therapy

In accordance with the American Psychological Association, cognitive behavior therapy (CBT) is the most well-studied treatment for the hoarding problem. CBT focuses on addressing the ideas and emotions that contribute to hoarding behavior. CBT teaches people how to identify the ideas and beliefs that cause them to save or accumulate goods. Gradually, the person learns to resist the impulse to buy or bring home more items.

People with the disease can acquire coping strategies that will help them make better judgments. For example, someone may consider the significance of decluttering their home based on safety and health considerations.

Motivational Interviewing

Motivational interviewing (MI) is another treatment option for hoarding problems. Motivational interviewing, according to the International OCD Foundation, entails addressing any doubts a person may have about identifying and changing their hoarding activity.

A therapist assists the patient in exploring goals and values while also analyzing their existing situation.

Motivational interviewing taps into a person's inherent desire to improve. It encourages a person to prioritize improving certain conduct and enhances their confidence in their ability to do so.

Group and Family Therapy
Many therapeutic regimens involve group and family therapy. Individuals with hoarding problems, as well as members of their support systems, can benefit from these approaches.

Harm Reduction for Hoarding Disorder

In recent years, specialists have proposed harm-reduction strategies for addressing hoarding disorders. Harm reduction aims to mitigate the consequences of high-risk conduct. It is not necessary for someone to change their behavior before receiving assistance. It meets them wherever they are.

In this type of treatment, the individual with hoarding disorder, their loved ones, and their therapist collaborate to address the problem. According to the Oxford Handbook of Hoarding and Acquiring, family-oriented harm reduction for hoarding entails increasing a patient and family's willingness to participate in treatment, identifying harm potential, forming a harm reduction team, and executing and managing a damage reduction strategy.

Recognize Hoarding Disorder Symptoms in Yourself

Hoarding problems can have a significant influence on your own and your loved ones' lives. Living with other family members can lead to substantial stress and conflict. The following tactics can help you stay on track in a treatment plan that you create with a mental health practitioner.

Stick with the Program
Remember that it is natural to experience setbacks. If your rehabilitation does not proceed as planned, do not be too hard on yourself. Trust that with time, practice, and assistance, you can improve.

Accept help
Mental health specialists can assist you in beginning your recovery journey. Consider enlisting the assistance of loved ones to help you stay on that path.

If you have relatives that are eager to assist you organize and tidy your living environment, please consider accepting. Often, friends and relatives want you to get better and are willing to help you get there.

Socialise
People suffering from hoarding disorder may become isolated due to feelings of shame and stigma. Take tiny steps to connect with others to enhance your outlook. If you are used to being alone, socializing may be difficult for you. If going out with a large gathering of people makes you uncomfortable, you don't have to do it.

Instead, invite one or two friends or family members to join you for lunch or a movie. By choosing low-key activities, you can gradually become accustomed to spending time with others. You can also look for support networks online to connect with other people who have hoarding disorder.

Practice self-care
If you have recently rediscovered your kitchen and bathroom, reintroduce yourself to self-care. Purchasing and preparing nutritious foods, taking regular baths, and enjoying your surroundings can all help to strengthen your determination. Of course, you will look and feel better, and as you gain confidence, consider inviting a family member or close friend over for a cup of coffee or a simple card game. This can drive you to keep your space clutter-free.

Consider the welfare of loved ones
People with hoarding problems may be unaware of the influence it has on their loved ones, such as parents, children, or pets. The disease can be stressful for both you and your loved ones. If hoarding is not addressed, family members may develop resentment, hostility, and, in some circumstances, depression. Children may suffer social consequences, and if living conditions are severe enough, family members may lose custody of children or pets.

Addressing hoarding to improve your family's quality of life can result in a much happier house and improved health conditions for everyone in the household.